Images of
Croydon

Images of
Croydon

Croydon Advertiser Group

The Breedon Books
Publishing Company
Derby

First published in Great Britain by
The Breedon Books Publishing Company Limited
44 Friar Gate, Derby, DE1 1DA.
1997

ISBN 1 85983 108 7

Printed and bound by Butler & Tanner, Frome, Somerset.
Jacket printed by Lawrence Allen Ltd, Weston-super-Mare, Somerset.
Colour film by RPS Ltd of Leicester.

Contents

Introduction

A LONG, long time ago people got their news from newspapers: they turned to the national newspapers for information about the major things in life while local newspapers dealt with the myriad of information from the areas where they lived and worked. It was the local newspaper's role to provide details about what local life was all about: from who was being born, who had died, what the local authority was planning, to who had won the top rosettes in the flower and produce shows.

We all had more time to read in those days: there was no pressure on us and the only real competition a local newspaper faced was from the public lending library: if you did not spend your time sitting down and flipping through the pages of the newspaper you would probably be flipping through the latest romance, thriller or autobiographical book added to the library's shelves.

Words were the main ingredient for newspapers and books: photographs were often there merely to break up the slabs of grey text on a printed page.

It is only in recent years that the news photographer's skill has increasingly come to the fore. The advent of the moving image on our television screens has meant that newspapers have had to look more closely at the ways in which photographs are captured and presented on a page. The photo-journalist's skill has been recognised.

But that skill is not new: it was always there. The trouble is it was not recognised as such.

In *Images of Croydon* we have the opportunity to revisit some of the early photographs taken to illustrate captured moments of time in Croydon's history: many of these photographs have been used in the *Croydon Advertiser* and similar local newspapers from the area that no longer exist. Others are from the collection of John Gent who has an unrivalled assortment of pictures from professional and amateur photographers who have captured the town and its people almost from the time the first cameras became available to a mass audience.

Together these images produce a fascinating glimpse of the charm and character of Croydon that still endures.

Malcolm J.Starbrook
Editor
Croydon Advertiser

Around the Town

Croydon High Street around 1890, with the second town hall on the left. The Ship public house remains but all the buildings on the left were demolished when the street was widened in the 1890s.

The medieval market area was a network of narrow streets and alleys and had become very run down by the late 19th century. Middle Row seen here was cleared away with most of the surrounding area in the early 1890s.

Market Street just before demolition.

Streeter's Hill about 1890.

Surrey Street, formerly Butcher Row, about 1890.

A horse tram stands outside the Green Dragon in the rather dusty High Street, 1896.

The old Parish Church and Palace of the Archbishops – Croydon's former Manor house.

The chapel of Croydon Palace, for centuries the country home of the Archbishops of Canterbury.

The gateway to Croydon Palace, demolished in the 1880s.

Horse trams in North End, with the Whitgift Hospital on the right, about 1885.

Looking north-east from the tower of the Parish Church, 1900.

Looking east from the tower of the Parish Church, 1900.

Croydon General Hospital in London Road around 1880.

A steam train passes as animals graze on the Fairfield around 1900. St Matthew's Church in George Street is on the left.

North End with an electric tram in 1908.

The audience chamber of the Whitgift Hospital, North End.

The Whitgift Middle School in North End was demolished in the mid-1960s and the site is now occupied by the Whitgift Shopping Centre.

London Road, with Tamworth Road to the right about 1908.

Busy North End looking towards West Croydon around 1908.

North End just after World War One.

North End. Admission to the Croydon Picture House was adults 6d and 3d, children 3d and 2d!

Trams dominate the junction of Tamworth Road, London Road and Station Road in 1909.

West Croydon Railway Bridge; you could stand and chat in the road in 1906.

The widened High Street around 1908. The Greyhound Hotel on the right was once Croydon's principal coaching inn but was demolished in the 1960s.

High Street in 1909.

South End: Most of the buildings on the right remain.

Katharine Street was graced with a rather fine mid-Victorian terrace on the left, demolished in the 1960s.

Wellesley Road appeared rather different in 1909 from the present day dual carriageway, underpass and tall office blocks.

East Croydon Station in 1910. The trams were scrapped in 1927 but modern ones should be running past the new station in 1999.

Church Street, with Surrey Street on the right.

The third town hall was opened in 1896; part of the building now houses a museum and arts complex, with a splendid new library at the back and is known as the Clocktower.

George Street in the late 1920s.

North End about 1927.

North End with the Scala Cinema on the right.

High Street in 1936.

High Street with the Davis Theatre on the right.

Busy Surrey Street Market still attracts many shoppers as it did in the 1930s.

You could park in North End whilst doing your Christmas shopping in 1935.

Like so many other towns, Croydon had its poorer districts and slums. In 1938 parts of the Old Town area were redeveloped.

Clearance of Leighton Street, 1938.

North End around 1947.

North End with plenty of trams around 1947.

High Street not long after World War Two.

Several of the High Street shops on the right still had temporary windows after wartime bomb damage when this picture was taken.

The Fairfield Halls were under construction in 1961 but the old cottages in Park Lane had not yet been demolished for road widening.

In the 1960s the local council started a massive redevelopment scheme. In 1963, St George's House, right was nearing completion: Essex House, left has since been demolished and the site awaits development.

Mr & Mrs Gough look at the changing face of Croydon. Norfolk House seen here was the first of the many office blocks in the town centre.

Essex House, George Street, under construction in 1961.

St Matthew's Church and the new church hall provided a rather fine contrast to Essex House in 1962. All three buildings have now gone!

In 1964 the railway bridge at East Croydon Station was widened. Work was also in hand on building a new Head Post Office and sorting office on the site adjacent to the station.

The Whitgift Centre opened in 1966 and has been completely covered and modernised in recent years. It is one of the largest shopping centres in the south-east.

The High Street, widened on the left in the 1890s, was partially widened again, but this time on the right, in the early 1960s. Some of London Transport's familiar RT and RM type buses complete the scene.

Around the Districts

The Crystal Palace dominated North Croydon from 1854 until its destruction by fire in 1936. It was just outside the borough but many Croydonians visited its exhibitions and other attractions in their leisure time.

Upper Norwood was just a remote settlement in the Great North Wood until the Crystal Palace came to the area and brought much housing development and new shops.

The Tram Terminus at Crystal Palace was at the point where four parishes met.

Brunel's twin towers of the Crystal Palace contained water tanks to provide adequate pressure for the many fountains and water features in the grounds. A trolleybus has replaced the trams, and is dwarfed by the South tower.

The Queen's Hotel in Church Road is still a local landmark.

Norbury was a country area at the northern extremity of Croydon until the electric trams arrived in 1901.

Not far from Norbury tram terminus, this rural aspect remained until after World War One.

These Edwardian children do not look very pleased at being photographed in Woodvale Avenue, South Norwood.

The Gaiety Cinema in South Norwood High Street was just one of many cinemas in Croydon.

Portland Road is one of South Norwood's main shopping streets.

The Stanley Halls at the bottom of South Norwood Hill was generously designed and donated by Mr William Ford Stanley, of Cumberlow, South Norwood.

Woodside Green still has a 'villagey' atmosphere and has not changed a great deal eighty years after this photograph.

Nicholson Road Addiscombe is typical of many residential streets in the town, but is now lined with parked cars.

Lower Addiscombe Road does not appear very different today, apart from the traffic, and the absence of the church on the left, burnt down shortly after World War Two. Addiscombe Station, right, closed in May 1997 as part of the Tramlink project.

A motor cyclist accelerates around the bend by the 'Black Horse' at Addiscombe.

Much of rural Croydon disappeared under suburban development in the 20th century, but often it was some time before the new roads were properly surfaced as in Ashburton Avenue.

The Croydon area was well-wooded so it is not surprising many of the local houses were built of wood. These old cottages in Shirley Road disappeared to be replaced by modern houses many years ago.

Whitehorse Road around 1910 with the tower of Gillett and Johnston's Bell Foundry on the left and the wooded Norwood Hills in the distance.

Horse-drawn traffic predominates in this view of Broad Green, but passengers on the relatively new electric tram are enjoying the sunshine.

Thornton Heath High Street with a splendid early motor car.

Thornton Heath High Street in the 1920s.

London Road around 1900, with the Congregational Church on the left.

Thornton Heath Station around 1905.

Children, some with hoops, line up for the photographer in Melfort Road, Thornton Heath.

Not a vehicle in sight shortly after the houses were built in Lyndhurst Road, Thornton Heath.

These old cottages were some of the oldest in Thornton Heath but were demolished just before World War Two.

The Lord Napier public house in Thornton Heath has for many years been famous as a jazz venue but was obviously popular ninety years ago.

Thornton Heath Pond was a well-known local landmark, but was filled in during 1953.

This wooden cottage in Colliers Water Lane disappeared many years ago but the name of the road is a reminder of an important local industry, charcoal burning, from the middle ages when Croydon supplied the City of London with its fuel.

In 1900 Thornton Road bore little resemblance to that of the present role – part of the A23 London to Brighton road.

The junction of Mitcham and Thornton Roads with Purley Way is much busier today than it was sixty years ago.

The River Wandle just on the Beddington side of Waddon Mill is still attractive, but the flow of water is much less and the river hardly a quarter of the width seen here.

Waddon Marsh Lane, photographed in 1900 became part of the town's by-pass, Purley Way, in the 1920s. The Hare and Hounds, left is still easily recognisable.

New housing is gradually encroaching on to the downs south of Purley in this view from the late Edwardian period.

Purley Cross is now the extremely busy junction of the A22 (Eastbourne) and A23 (Brighton) roads. Around 1903 however it still had a fairly rural air although new buildings were coming on the scene.

An early view of Purley Tram Terminus before the shops were built in the Brighton Road, replacing the houses seen here.

Purley Tram Terminus around 1909.

Houses were gradually spreading over the rolling downland between Purley and Coulsdon just before World War One.

Godstone Road, with Riddlesdown on the left and the Kenley Hotel on the right.

Sanderstead Village remained as an isolated settlement high on the North Downs until housing development in the late 1920s and early 1930s.

Despite the arrival of new houses in Purley Oaks Road, corn was still being harvested in the fields opposite in the 1920s.

Selsdon developed when late 1920s housing and shops arrived on the scene to disturb its hitherto rural tranquillity.

Shirley was ripe for 1920s and 1930s development and soon grew into an attractive suburban area.

Addington was one of the last areas close to Croydon town centre to lose its rural aspect. In 1937 only a Croydon Corporation lamp post and two somewhat conflicting traffic signs suggested that rural Lodge Lane was not in a completely isolated part of the country.

An aerial view of new housing at New Addington a few years before World War Two.

In 1945 one could easily walk down the middle of Spout Hill into Addington Village without fear of an approaching motor vehicle.

New housing was urgently needed after World War Two. The Sylvan Estate at Upper Norwood was just one of a number to occupy some of the remaining open parts of the town.

At Work

Hard manual work was the order of the day in Victorian and Edwardian times.

Farming was an important local industry until relatively recent times, and employed many workers before mechanisation as seen here at Waddon in 1907.

Farmworkers loading hay on to a cart at Park Hill around 1908.

This fine cow, Mayflower, belonged to Mr Parsons of Addiscombe Farm and was a prize-winner at Croydon Horse Show in 1908.

A single row seed drill in use near Thornton Road in 1911.

Waddon Mill ground corn until 1928, one of the last working water mills on the River Wandle.

The Croydon Volunteer Fire Brigade pose for the photographer in the 1870s.

A fine turn out of the Fire Brigade at Park Lane before mechanisation.

The South Norwood Fire Station had space for only one machine, seen here next to the Stanley Halls.

Testing a newly delivered fire engine at Woodside Fire Station in 1937.

Postal workers pose outside the large Norwood Post Office in Westow Street around 1912.

In 1908 Coulsdon was still a village and in contrast, the Post Office was then the only shop there.

The *Croydon Advertiser* was established by Jesse Ward in 1869. The compositors' room was very busy in 1900.

The *Croydon Advertiser* offices at 36 High Street remained little changed from this 1930s view until the move to Brighton Road in the mid 1960s.

Thomas Wheeler was obviously proud of his staff and delivery vehicles so had their photograph taken opposite his Mitcham Road premises.

This splendid hand delivery cart was photographed in South Croydon.

The Whitgift Dairies had several shops in the town apart from this one in Brighton Road.

Inside the United Dairies' shop in Whitehorse Road.

Marks and Spencer's first Croydon shop opened in London Road in 1906.

Wilson's Tea Warehouse and cafe at 7 North End was a popular rendezvous for over seventy years. This is their tea cutting, blending and equalising machinery.

Polhill's shop in South End had a splendid display of meat and poultry. Present day Environmental Health inspectors might not approve.

Joshua Allder established his shop in North End in 1862, and by the 1930s this arcade had been built; it is now Allder's Mall.

Corporation staff busily engaged at the new electric tram depot and workshops in London Road, Thornton Heath around 1906.

A World War One scene with women conductors at Thornton Heath tram depot.

Building the new motor bus garage at Brighton Road, South Croydon in 1916.

John Horrocks' joinery works at Oval Road, Croydon.

The staff of Abner Creasy's, at the firm's Pembury Road coach building works in South Norwood.

Creasey's staff at work on Welford's dairy carts around 1914.

Gillett and Johnston's Bell Foundry and Clock Works at Union Road had a world-wide reputation. Staff are preparing inside and outside moulds for bells.

One of the bells cast for the Metropolitan Methodist Church in Toronto in 1922.

Seven hundred clocks were supplied to the London County Council for County Hall at Westminster. This photograph shows 100 of them, with a Master clock.

During World War One, National Aircraft Factory Number One was built at Waddon, employing some 2,000 people. This is the fuselage and plane erecting department.

Waddon Marsh Halt on the West Croydon to Wimbledon railway line was never a very busy station but the coal traffic to the adjacent electricity power stations and the gas works resulted in it having probably the heaviest freight movement on the Southern Region of British Railways. This 1971 scene is almost unrecognisable today and the railway closed in May 1997 for conversion to a light railway as part of Croydon Tramlink.

A contrasting scene in 1987, with horses grazing alongside the disused Croydon 'B' Power Station. Only the two large chimneys now remain and superstores occupy most of the site and surrounding area.

Gillett and Johnston provided good facilities for their staff including a canteen, and tennis courts behind the factory.

Getting About

The romance of coaching days is occasionally recreated by enthusiasts such as these near Thornton Heath Pond around 1937.

This baker's cart of Thornberry and Son is typical of those common in most towns until the 1950s.

A Croydon Tramway's Company horse tram in London Road, probably in the 1890s.

Workers laying track for the new electric trams in North End in 1901.

Croydon Corporation Tramway's employees at Thornton Heath Depot.

Trams and 1930s fashions in North End outside Allders.

Trolleybuses replaced trams on the routes to Crystal Palace, Sutton and Tooting during the 1930s. This wartime view shows a trolleybus in Tamworth Road, soon to see trams again after more than sixty years.

The last trams in Croydon ran in April 1951, seen off by huge crowds.

In 1953 the tram tracks were removed from Brighton Road, near the Windsor Castle Public House.

The Swan and Sugar Loaf is a well-known local landmark and its appearance has changed little in 100 years, but the early motor buses seen here have long gone.

One of Thomas Tilling's petrol electric motor buses outside the Swan and Sugar Loaf.

Despite the drizzle, members of the Jolly Boys' outing club are ready to set off by char-a-banc from the Kenley Hotel in 1921.

Two of Thomas Tilling's motor buses pass at Purley around 1931.

The Red Deer in Brighton Road is a well-known local landmark looking much the same in 1996 as it did here in the early 1930s.

A splendid line up of cycles outside the Addiscombe Garage and Cycle works.

The motor car was becoming popular by the 1930s and used cars were already sought after.

As traffic increased many roads had to be widened. Marlpit Lane was completely closed in 1937 for this to be done.

Croydon has an important place in the history of railways and East Croydon is its principal station. The *Croydon Advertiser* was well publicised in this view from some eighty years ago.

Purley Oaks signal box and station staff in the early 1900s.

For some years before introduction of third rail electrification in the area, overhead wires were used. Here an electric train is at Windmill Bridge Junction in the late 1920s.

The locomotive depot at West Croydon still had plenty of steam engines in 1925 despite the electrification of some trains.

In 1935 Bingham Road station was reopened following electrification of the line between Woodside and Selsdon. The line was closed again in 1983, and will form part of the Croydon Tramlink system from 1999.

In 1921 Croydon Aerodrome – Britain's first continental airport appeared rather basic!

An aerial view of Croydon Airport in the early 1920s.

An Air Union Passenger saloon, complete with steward, in the early 1920s.

Croydon Aerodrome soon outgrew its original site and was enlarged, with new terminal buildings on the newly opened Croydon By-Pass, Purley Way, in 1928.

Arrival of the first air mail at Croydon from Perth in Australia on 3 October 1938.

The interior of the Croydon Airport Control Tower in 1930.

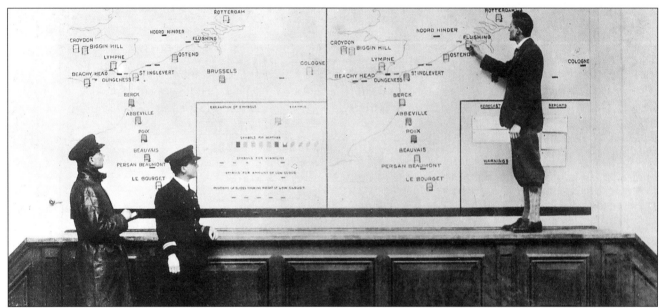

The Air Ministry weather chart at
Croydon Airport.

One of the famous
Handley Page HP42s flies
above the airport and
Purley Way in the early
1930s.

At Play

Croham Hurst has for generations been a popular spot for Croydonians. These cheeky Edwardian boys seem to be enjoying the pebbly hillside.

A wintry view looking west from the summit of Croham Hurst. The spread of vegetation has now spoilt much of the view.

Croydonians enjoy a walk in wintry sunshine near Croham Hurst around 1910.

The boating lake in Wandle Park attracted many Croydonians but sadly was filled in after bomb damage in World War Two.

Addington Hills, or as they are better known locally, Shirley Hills were and still are a popular venue for Croydonians and South Londoners on a fine day. Encroaching Silver Birch has covered most of the hills today.

Tea Gardens were available at Shirley for day trippers.

The last fair to be held on Shirley Hills was in March 1938.

The downs south of Croydon have long attracted visitors. The Pleasure Gardens at Riddlesdown catered for thousands of visitors on Bank Holidays and fine Sundays during the Edwardian Period.

The Town Hall Gardens, now enlarged as part of the Queen's Gardens, are a pleasant oasis in the town centre.

Park Hill was one of the town's first public parks, opened in July 1888 during a snowstorm!

Bandstands such as this at Thornton Heath Recreation Ground were a feature of most parks until after World War Two.

Grange Wood at Thornton Heath has always been popular in a densely populated part of the town with few open spaces.

The Bowling Green at Grange Wood is one of many around the town, and the Croydon Bowling Club claims to be one of the oldest in the country.

Two Edwardian ladies read near the drinking fountain in Grange Wood.

Shirley Park Golf Club still flourishes but the club house is a newer building than that seen here and looks rather different.

Purley Downs Golf Club is one of many on the hills south of Croydon.

August 1938 and the opening of the new season was marked by the signing of James Bryson from the Scottish side, Morton Senior.

Palace won 6-2 when playing Hitchin in November 1960.

The Crystal Palace Football Club is Croydon's local team and this photograph shows a section of the crowd at Selhurst Park whe

ney beat Swindon Town 5-1 on Boxing Day 1935.

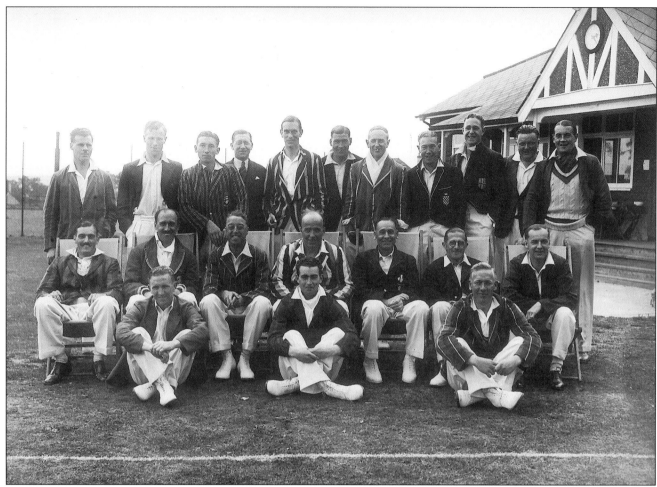

In July 1936 some famous players visited Addiscombe Cricket Club during its Home Week. Here the legendary Jack Hobbs, his son, and P.H.G.Fender have joined the local members.

The Kenley Police Comic Football Team made a fine line up in 1914, but the presence of firearms appears questionable.

The Upper Norwood Literary Society enjoyed an evening of reminiscences of Norwood from this be-whiskered group of local inhabitants on 10 April 1907.

The Croydon Natural History and Scientific Society still flourishes some 100 years after this excursion by a group of its members.

The Thornton Heath Tradesman's Dance in 1913.

The large Davis Theatre hosted film and stage shows during its thirty years of existence.

The Grand Theatre and Opera House was a early Victorian theatre and the venue for many happy evenings during its sixty years in the High Street.

In 1938 the famous organist, Reginald Foort, appeared at the Croydon Empire in North End. His portable organ is here being delivered to the theatre.

Croydon Repertory Theatre was justly famed in the 1930s. This garden party was arranged by the theatre in July 1937.

Following the closure of the Davis and Grand Theatres in 1959 a brave new theatrical venture was launched. The Pembroke Theatre (in the round) opened in October 1959, with *Thieves Carnival* pictured here on the opening night. Unfortunately the theatre only survived for a short time when cinemas and theatres everywhere were losing audiences.

In the absence through indisposition of Sir Thomas Beecham, it was Dr Malcolm Sargent who conducted the London Philharmonic Orchestra at the North End Hall in 1938.

Entertainment at the Queen's Gardens on a fine day in 1987.

A group of young Croydonians enjoy half burying one of their mates on the 'beach' at Purley Way Pool in 1936.

The late Arthur Davison was probably the town's principal music maker in the 1970s and '80s and is seen here conducting a rehearsal of the Croydon Technical College Youth Orchestra in 1973.

The Open Air Swimming Pool at Purley Way opened in 1935 and proved very popular on fine days. It was closed some years ago and is now a garden centre.

Croydon's People

In the garden of 236 London Road around 1900.

The Whitgift Hospital has stood at the junction of North End and George Street since 1596 and still provides shelter for the elderly. This view shows some Edwardian residents.

Croydon School of Art was housed in the Public Halls in George Street where these ladies were under instruction.

The Gordon Boys' Home founded in 1885 in Croydon Grove had moved to Morland Road when Major General Baden Powell paid a visit.

The Whitehorse Mission Room was in one of the poorer parts of town.

The woodwork class in a Thornton Heath School around ninety years ago.

Mark Ward in Croydon General Hospital seems well supplied with flowers and plants.

The Gospel Temperance Hall in Mint Walk was home to one of the many bands in the town.

South Croydon Salvation Army band in 1928.

Commuters at Thornton Heath Station wait for the 8.10am train to Victoria. All are wearing hats!

The North End Hall, home to the North End Brotherhood, was purchased by the Corporation and became the Civic Hall during World War Two, and was replaced by the Fairfield Halls in 1962.

The junior room at Ashburton Library around 1927.

The Women's League of Health and Beauty put on this display at St Peter's Hall, South Croydon in 1930.

'Paper Jack' was a much loved Croydon eccentric who insisted on clothing himself in newspapers and living in open spaces in the Waddon and Beddington areas. He was killed by a motor car in 1935, but older Croydonians still remember him with affection.

Some of Miss Doris Austin's pupils demonstrating rhythmic movement and their percussion band at Sanderstead Council School in 1943.

Margaret Lockwood was the glamorous visitor surrounded by a bevy of nurses at Croydon General Hospital in 1959.

Maurice Chevalier takes an afternoon nap at the Selsdon Park Hotel in 1963.

Sir James Marshall was largely responsible for masterminding the commercial redevelopment of Croydon in the 1960s. He received the Freedom of the Borough in a Town Hall ceremony.

Many homes in Croydon were without bathrooms until after World War Two but home improvements ended the need for public slipper baths and wash houses such as this at Windmill Road which closed in 1963.

It Was News Then

The Duchess of Albany inaugurates Purley Fountain in 1904.

Croydon Lifeboat day in July 1908. Part of the procession turns out of Brigstock Road into London Road at Thornton Heath.

Sports at Woodside in 1907.

The aftermath of the Stoats Nest railway disaster in 1910. The station was subsequently renamed Coulsdon North and was closed in 1983.

The opening Ceremony at Purley Cottage Hospital in March 1909.

Horses come to the rescue of a Royal Mail Parcel motor van which has broken down in the Brighton Road.

Members of the Boy's Brigade on a church parade in North End.

The Lord Bishop of Southwark turning the first sod at the site of St Andrew's Church, Coulsdon, in 1913.

Croydon Postal District Church Parade in Rectory Grove, 1912.

Whitgift Grammar School boys march to the Parish Church for Founder's Day service, 1911.

Field Marshall Earl Roberts presenting Colours to the 4th Battalion Queen's Royal Regiment at Duppas Hill.

The Mayoress, Mrs Southwell, selling roses on Alexandra Day, 1924.

The Mayoress presents an address to the Mayor, Alderman Howard Houlder on Women's Citizen's Day 1918, in celebration of franchise reform.

The Mayor, Alderman Southwell, opening a railwaymen's fete at The Nest, Selhurst.

The Mayor at the Annual Church Parade of the Croydon and District Friendly Society and Trade Unions in aid of the Croydon General Hospital and Surrey Convalescent Homes, 1924.

At the League of Nations Dance at the Baths Hall in 1924.

West Croydon Wesleyan Church Children's Treat 1925.

The Mayor, Alderman Southwell, presents a cheque for £10, and a framed 'Roll of Honour' certificate to Mr Ernest Hart of Southsea who, while lodging in Croydon, saved a mother and child from a runaway horse in George Street, 1925.

The Mayor, Alderman Southwell at the Croydon Times' Children's Ball held in the Winter Gardens, Scarbrook Road in 1925.

The Mayor releases a balloon to open a fete at The Nest, 1925.

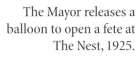

The Prince of Wales and the Mayor, Alderman Southwell, at the opening of Norwood Grove as a public park in 1926.

The Prince of Wales declares Norwood Grove open, 1926.

Queen Mary arrives at the Whitgift school in 1938.

Crowds, apparently undeterred by the weather, eagerly await the opening of the new Co-op store in London Road in 1938.

Crowds waiting for the arrival of Amy Johnson and Jim Mollison at Croydon Airport in 1936.

Amy Johnson and Jim Mollison make their way through crowds after their flight from South Africa.

Miss Norah Swinburne, the actress signs autographs at Messrs Grant Brothers' department store in celebration of their sixty yea

f trading, 1937.

The Crystal Palace ablaze in November 1936, as one of the most spectacular fires in memory engulfed the famous building.

Workmen clear the ruins of the Crystal Palace some time after the fire in 1936.

Kennard's Department Store in North End was the scene of many entertaining events. In September 1936 one of the more bizarre was the escape of Joss, a baboon. Here his keeper attempts to recapture him.

Crowds stand outside Allder's store watching Joss on Kennard's roof.

Miss Norah Buttram and Mr Fred Cliffe, two midgets who were appearing at the Grand Theatre, photographed after their wedding in Croydon in 1936.

The Prince of Wales about to embark on a flight to Copenhagen from Croydon Airport in 1932.

Cinema workers demonstrate outside the massive Davis Theatre in Croydon High Street.

The Streets of Adventure Carnival in High Street 1937.

The last interment at Croydon's old Parish Church of St John the Baptist. The church is the burial place of six Archbishops of Canterbury from the 16th, 17th and 18th centuries.

Coronation illuminations in Katharine Street, 1937.

Surrey Street market traders celebrate the 1937 Coronation.

A 1937 Coronation party in Coldharbour Lane, Waddon.

The Empire Air Display at Kenley Aerodrome in 1937.

The Fourth Queen's Regiment march through George Street.

Whitgift pupils act as newspaper sellers.

New Addington prides itself on its annual carnival. Here the 1956 event has attracted good crowds.

An electric train shot through the buffers at West Croydon Station in 1948, fortunately without injury to any passengers, but left one or two cars in the adjacent car park looking somewhat the worse for wear.

Sir Winston Churchill enters South Norwood Conservative Club, followed by Vice-Admiral John Hughes-Hallett, a candidate (later successful) for the local by-election in 1954.

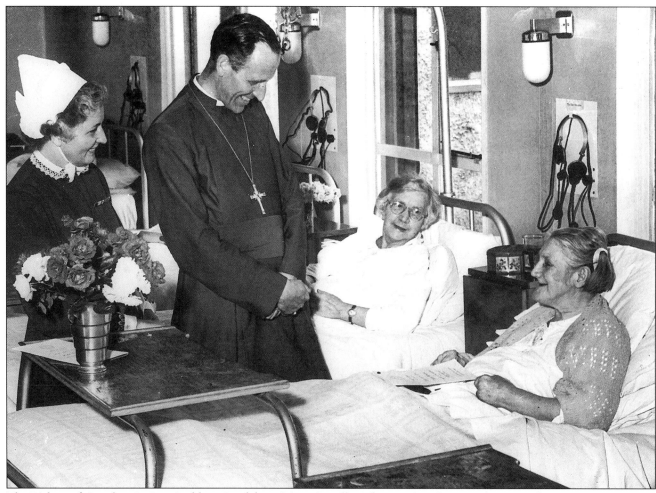

The Bishop of Croydon, Rt Rev Cuthbert Bardsley, visits Miss Ella Cole, a patient in Queen's Hospital in 1951.

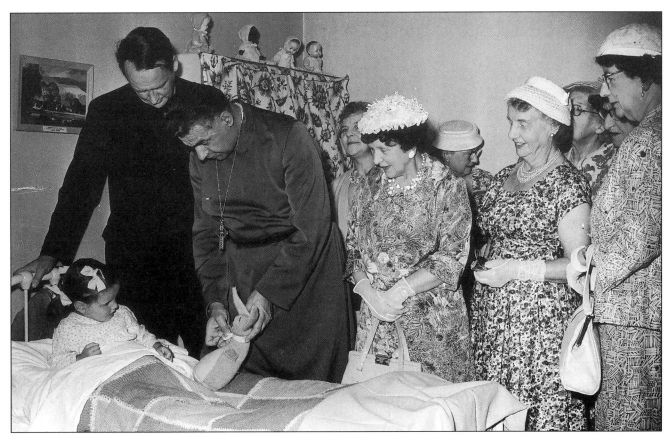

The Bishop, Rt Rev John Hughes, chats with a young girl after dedicating the bed she occupied at Dr Barnardo's home in Pampisford Road.

The Archbishop of Canterbury, Dr Michael Ramsey, lays the foundation stone of the new Trinity School of John Whitgift at Shirley Park in 1964.

The Queen and the Duke of Edinburgh arrive at the Town Hall in 1960 as part of the town's Millenary Celebrations to mark 1,000 years of recorded history.

Queen Elizabeth, the Queen Mother receives a bouquet from David Aston, son of the Mayor and Mayoress, at the opening of the Fairfield Halls in 1962.

A 50-ton mobile crane places one of 18 beams across the High Street as construction of the new flyover progresses in 1967.

Crowds watch the fire which badly damaged the long-established shop premises of Messrs Hewitt's in Church Street.

The last pony ride in Kennard's arcade, 1966. There were surely not many shops where children could have had such a happy time.

In 1983 Croydon celebrated its centenary as a borough and received a royal visit. Her Majesty the Queen is here talking to local residents.

As part of the celebration, the Queen formally opened the extended Town Hall Gardens and named them The Queen's Gardens. The Mayor, Margaret Campbell and the Town Clerk, Frank Birch, are with Her Majesty.

The electrification of the Sanderstead to East Grinstead railway line was celebrated in style by Bob Bates and the Barra Boys as they serenaded Transport Secretary Paul Channon, Foreign Secretary Sir Geoffrey Howe, and MP Tim Renton at Sanderstead station in 1987.

A spectacular rail crash at Purley in 1989 sadly left some dead and injured.

One of the coaches is lifted high over the houses in Glenn Avenue, Purley, as the wreckage is cleared after the accident.

A large crowd processes along London Road, Norbury in 1990 to object to road building proposals and plead for better public transport.

The Mayor, Councillor Dudley Mead met his opposite member from Lambeth at the boundary between the two boroughs.

A suspected bomb on a bus caused chaos in Brighton Road in March 1997.

War and Peace

Wilford Road is decorated to celebrate the end of the Boer war in 1900. The building on the left remains but all the others were cleared away in the 1960s and the road no longer exists.

The Territorials were mobilised on 5 August 1914 and are seen in London Road by Oakfield Road.

Several local schools were used as hospitals during World War One. This is the prize band at Ingram Road War Hospital, Thornton Heath in 1916.

The kitchen at Stanford Road War Hospital, Norbury in 1918.

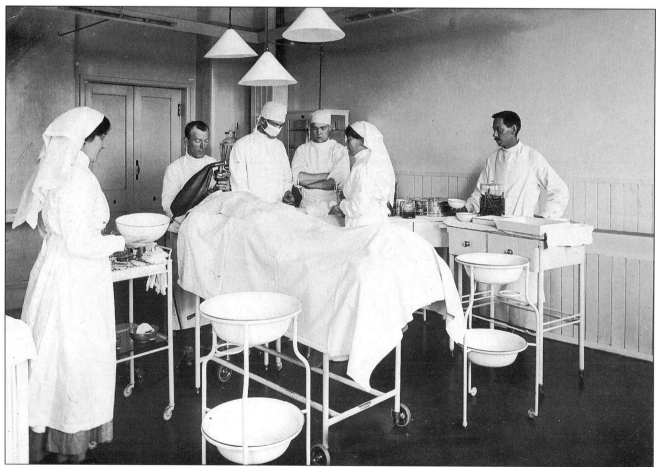

The Operating Theatre at the Crescent War Hospital.

The Crescent War Hospital.

Fire practice at Addington Palace War Hospital, 1915.

Helpers raising money for the Croydon Gas Company's War Comforts Fund.

Croydon's great 1916 Recruiting Rally was intended to appeal to the large numbers of young men who had 'held back' up to the present! Here the procession is leaving St James's Road and turning into London Road at Broad Green.

A Whist Drive for wounded soldiers at the Town Hall Gardens in 1917.

The Croydon Gas Company Sports Ground was the venue for wounded soldiers to enjoy tea in the sunshine.

Outside the pavilion at the Gas Company's Sports Ground.

The losing side in the tug-of-war. It is to be hoped no further injuries occurred to the already wounded soldiers!

The funeral cortège of a Croydon soldier, killed on duty, leaves St Edmund's Church, Wandle Park.

Many Belgian refugees found sanctuary in Croydon during World War One. Here nuns and their young charges enjoy a trip to Shirley Hills – one of the town's favourite open spaces.

Peace Day crowds throng Katharine Street in 1919.

The unveiling of Croydon's War Memorial in Katharine Street, 22 October 1921.

The British Legion Festival of Remembrance at the Davis Theatre in the High Street, November 1938.

Territorials in George Street not long before World War Two.

A great two-mile long procession took place on 6 May 1939. Intended to encourage people to train for their country's defence, it was watched by thousands of Croydonians and part is seen here turning from Tamworth Road into London Road.

An exercise in dealing with incendiary bombs at Lorne Avenue, Shirley, 1939.

An air-raid precautions first aid exercise.

Recruiting for the ARP service at Woodside Green, 1939.

ARP Wardens on parade at Dingwall Avenue.

A Civil Defence
Parade.

Providing protection for the control centre at the Town Hall.

Distribution of tin hats, probably at Ashburton Park.

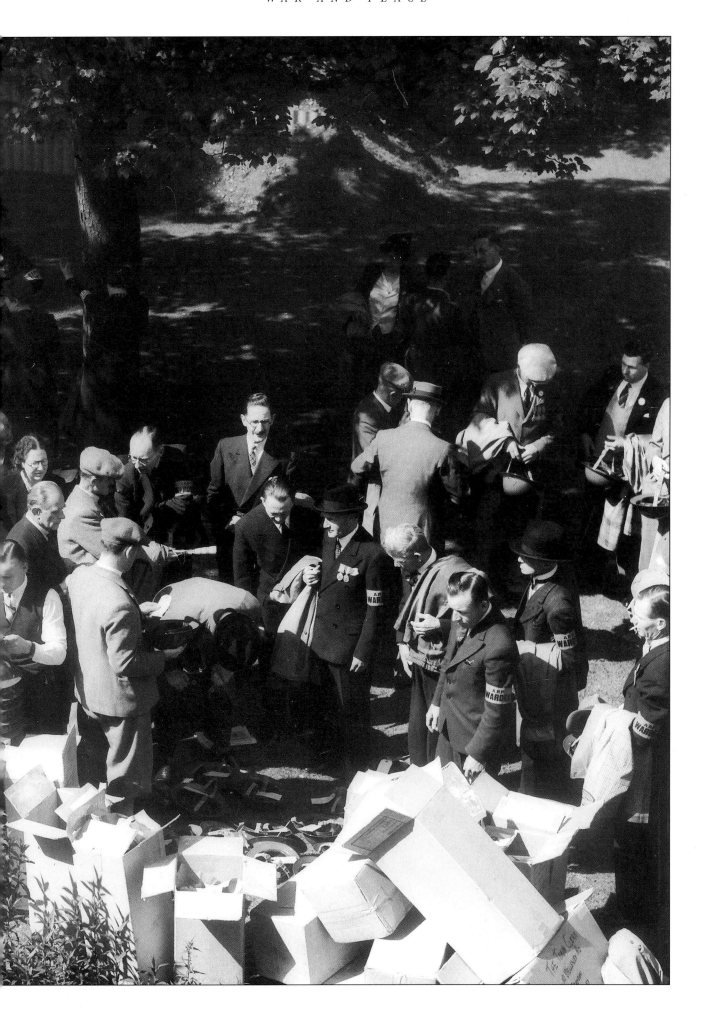

A police call box is well surrounded by sand bags.

A Civil Defence exercise at Fairfield car park.

Erecting an Anderson Shelter in a Croydon back garden, 1939.

Gas practice fortunately proved unnecessary but the fear of possible attack lasted for some time.

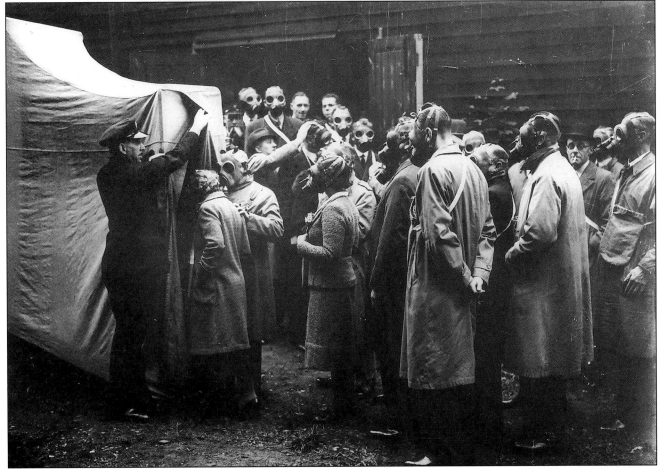

Preparing for evacuation, September 1939.

Fond farewells at Croydon Barracks in Mitcham Road as troops leave for war.

National Savings week 1940 saw the Mayor, Alderman Harding, and the Town Clerk, Ernest Taberner purchasing certificates, watched by Rear Admiral Harrison (left), Frank Roberts (right) and Miss Morgan.

On 15 August 1940, German aircraft attacked Croydon Airport, causing serious damage, killing 62 people, seriously injuring 37 and less seriously injuring 137. It was a foretaste of what was to come over the next four years. Here damaged houses on the nearby Waddon Estate seem to have survived serious structural damage.

The burial service for victims of the Croydon Airport raid was held a few days later at Mitcham Road Cemetery. Conducted by the Bishop Rt Rev Maurice Harland, it took place as sirens were sounding and fighters were in action overhead.

Members of the Local Defence Volunteers pass Thornton Heath Clock Tower in 1940. The LDV later became the Home Guard – Dad's Army.

A Christmas Party in an air-raid shelter at Woodville Road, Thornton Heath, 1940.

Wardens of an ARP reporting post in a private house gather in the front garden for group photograph.

An ARP auxiliary ambulance, probably at Mayday Hospital.

Admiral Sir Edward Evans at a Civil Defence demonstration on Fairfield Car Park, 1941.

Troops of all three services were stationed in the area and here a group partake of refreshments in North End.

Emergency static water tanks such as this in Windmill Grove, were installed at strategic points to aid fire-fighting.

Salvage was a priority during World War Two. Residents queue in a Croydon street to hand in books during one of the periodic 'Book Drives' to salvage waste paper. Unfortunately many historic documents were lost as a result!

A Corporation dustcart
is dwarfed by Croydon
Power Station as salvage
is sorted, 1940.

The cooling towers of
Croydon Power Station
were being carefully
camouflaged when this
picture was taken,
though whether it
fooled any German
bomber pilots is
doubtful.

The Queen pays a wartime visit to Croydon to hear something of the town's ordeal.

Group Captain John ('Cats Eyes') Cunningham pays a visit to his home town to present a plaque to the Mayor, Alderman Sam Roden, in recognition of the success of Wings for Victory Week, 1943.

Scaring birds at Purley Way in 1943.

The Bishop, The Rt Rev Maurice Harland is by the fire in the Parish Church Vestry, 1944, with some colleagues whilst resting from fire watching duty.

Croydon was particularly badly hit by V1s, (the Flying Bombs or 'Doodle Bugs') in 1944. One fell in Ross Road, South Norwood and Mr Henry Willinck (MP), his wife, and Alan Holt, Deputy Borough Engineer (left) inspect the damage and talk to residents.

A local housewife serves welcome cups of tea to rescue workers at The Crescent in July 1944, after a V1 incident.

Emergency street baths were provided when the flying bomb attacks were at their worst, as the public baths had been damaged and many houses had been wrecked or made uninhabitable.

A queue waits patiently to be served at a damaged butcher's shop in North End, 1944. 'Business as Usual' was a very common sign during the war, sometimes in the most incongruous situations!

The end of the European War in May 1945 was a cause for great rejoicing. Here a small crowd gather round a street bonfire to celebrate VE (Victory in Europe) Day.

Part of the vast crowd which gathered in the town centre on 15 August 1945, to celebrate VJ (Victory over Japan) Day. The war was over but Croydon had lost many of its sons and daughters.

Storms and Floods

The rural Shirley Inn, Wickham Road photographed on a wintry day around 1907. Building development in the 1930s brought this district into suburbia but the public house is little altered.

The great storm of the 14 June 1914 caused flooding in parts of the district as this view in London Road, Norbury, demonstrates.

Many parts of the South of England were snowbound in December 1927 after Boxing Day blizzards. Villages to the south of Croydon, such as Chaldon, Tatsfield, Farleigh and Chelsham were cut off for almost a week, by drifts of between 10 and 15 feet deep. Marlpit Lane, Coulsdon, seen here lost its rural appearance as a result of 1930s housing development.

The lower end of Marlpit Lane seen a few days later after most of the snow had melted. Floods occurred quite generally as a result of the rapid thaw of the deep snow.

The southern parts of Croydon, and the centre of Purley were prone to serious flooding because of the steep hills leading into the valley. In 1936, a local resident is attempting to clear blocked drains in South End near the Swan and Sugar Loaf public house.

Only the previous year similar conditions prevailed in one of the side streets off South End.

A bulldozer clears snow in Croydon High Street, 27 December 1962.

The 1962-63 winter was extremely severe, with snow lying for 10 weeks, and seven-foot drifts in parts of Croydon. The short road at Shirley Hills opposite Bishop's Walk was closed to traffic and used as a dump for snow.

The front drive of a house in Selsdon Road, Addington in January 1963.

Severe weather in January 1987 caused many problems on roads such as this – Selsdon Road, South Croydon.

Not for nothing is New Addington known as 'Little Siberia'. Its exposed position 500 feet up on the North Downs means that snowfall often causes problems. Residents are seen here queuing for food supplies and using toboggans in January 1987.

Another New Addington scene in January 1987.

Peter (left) and Stephen Bagatti (right) built this snowman outside their Park Lane restaurant in the town centre on 13 January 1987.

Residents of Dorrington Court, South Norwood Hill built this snowman in February 1981.

The great storms of October 1987 caused havoc in Croydon. Well over 50,000 trees toppled, and many roads were blocked. This scene in Addington Road, Selsdon was typical of many around the town.

Despite expensive flood prevention work, occasional freak downpours can cause problems as happened in August 1981 when Purley, seen here and other parts of the borough experienced flooding.

Pedestrianised North End was transformed by this early 1990s snowfall.

Recent Times

Office development between the 1960s and 1980s has given Croydon a dramatic skyline, seen here looking north in 1991 with the Fairfield Halls and Croydon College in the right foreground. *Photograph courtesy of Handfords.*

The Fairfield Halls seen across the Queen's Gardens in 1995.

North End is now an attractive pedestrianised street. The tower of the Town Hall is a prominent landmark in the distance.

Park Lane, and the underpass now takes most of the north-south traffic through the town.

Wellesley Road and the underpass are lined with office blocks – a far cry from the quiet winding road of the 1950s.

East Croydon station is a futuristic structure built on the suspension bridge principle as the actual bridge was not substantial enough to bear the weight of the size of building needed.

Croydon has many attractive open spaces including formal parks, woods and open downland. Happy Valley and Farthing Down in Coulsdon provide a marked contrast with the busier parts of town.

Bradmore Green at Coulsdon is in one of Croydon's Conservation Areas.

Addington Village is only three miles from the Town Hall. Five Archbishops of Canterbury are buried in the churchyard.

Tramlink, the light rail scheme for the Croydon area was developed in the 1980s and in 1991 this mock up of part of a new Sheffield tram was exhibited in the Queen's Gardens in the town centre.

Work on the Tramlink scheme started in September 1996 with the diversion of underground pipes, cables and sewers. Councillor Geraint Davis, leader of the Council, is launching a poster designed by Katie Gibbs.

Work on Tramlink was in full swing at Park Lane and elsewhere by mid-1997. The 28km system will include street running in the town centre, several sections of underused or disused railway lines and new alignments, serving Wimbledon, Beckenham, Elmers End and New Addington. It is expected to commence operating in 1999.